Want to make a warm wrap for yourself or one of your favorite friends or relatives, but don't have a lot of time? Then just get out your crochet hook and choose one of these fabulous throws which you can crochet in a weekend.

I0892956

LEISURE ARTS, INC.
Maumelle, Arkansas

Produced by
CREATIVE PARTNERS, LLC

Production Team
Pattern Testers: Kimberly Britt and
Patricia Honaker
Technical Editor: Mary Ann Frits
Book Design: Linda Causee

We have made every effort to ensure that these instructions are accurate and complete. We cannot, however, be responsible for human error, typographical mistakes or variations in individual work.

Published by Leisure Arts, Inc.

LEISURE ARTS
the art of everyday living

10

12

14

16

18

20

22

SHINING SHELLS

Finished Size: 33" x 52" (81.28 cm x 132.08 cm)

EASY

SHOPPING LIST

Yarn (Bulky Weight) 5

[3.5 ounces, 127 yards, (100 grams, 116 meters) per skein]

15 skeins

Crochet Hook

Size N (10 mm) crochet hook or size required for gauge

GAUGE INFORMATION

10 dc = 4" (10.16 cm)

STITCH GUIDE

Special Shell Stitch: Insert hook from front to back to front around post (vertical bar) of specified dc; work shell of (sc, hdc, 2 dc) around post.

THROW INSTRUCTIONS

Ch 131.

Row 1: Sc in 2nd ch from hook and in each ch: 130 sc, ch 1, turn.

Row 2: Sc in each sc, ch 3 (counts as first dc of next row thoughout), turn.

Row 3: Dc in each sc, ch 3, turn.

Row 4 (right side): Sc in first dc, sc in next dc, work shell around post of same dc; *skip 2 dc, sc in next dc, shell around post of same dc; rep from * across, sc in last 2 dc; ch 1, turn: 130 sts.

Row 5: Sc in each skipped dc and in each sc; ch 1, turn.

Row 6: Sc in each sc, ch 3, turn.

Repeat Rows 3 through 6 for desired length, ending by working Row 6. At end of last row, work 3 sc in last sc for corner.

EDGING

Rnd 1: Work sc across next long side, bottom, opposite side and top working 3 sc in each rem corner and taking care to keep work flat; join to beg sc.

Rnd 2: Ch 1, do not turn. * Skip 2 sc, in next sc work (sc, hdc, 2 dc); rep from * across, ending skip 2 sc, join in first sc. Finish off; weave in ends.

WONDERFUL WARMTH

Finished Size: 34" x 52" (86.36 cm x 132.08 cm)

EASY

SHOPPING LIST

Yarn (Bulky Weight) 5

[3.5 ounces, 129 yards (100 grams, 118 meters) per skein]

9 skeins

Crochet Hook

Size N (10 mm) crochet hook or size required for gauge

GAUGE INFORMATION

11 dc = 5" (12.7 cm)

THROW INSTRUCTIONS

Ch 122.

Row 1: Sc in 2nd ch from hook and in each rem ch: 121 sc; ch 3 (counts as first dc of following row throughout), turn; throw is worked lengthwise.

Row 2: Dc in each sc, ch 3, turn.

Row 3: Dc in each dc, ch 3, turn.

Repeat Row 3 until piece measures 34" (86.36 cm) long. At end of last row, ch 1, turn.

Last row: Sc in each dc. Finish off; weave in ends.

Fringe: Work across each short side edge of throw as follows: On right side of work, attach yarn at corner sc in first sc row, *ch 10, sc over post of end dc on next row, ch 5, sc over post of next dc; rep from * across side edge, ending with sc in last sc row. Finish off.

SENSATIONAL STRIPES

Finished Size: 35" x 50" (88.9 cm x 127 cm)

EASY

SHOPPING LIST

Yarn (Super Bulky) 6

[5 ounces, 153 yards (140 grams, 140 meters) per skein]

Red (A) - 4 skeins

White (B) - 3 skeins

Crochet Hook

Size N (10 mm) crochet hook or size required for gauge

GAUGE INFORMATION

In pattern, one sc + 3 chs = 1" (2.54 cm)

3 rows = 1" (2.54 cm)

CHANGING COLORS: To change colors, work sc until 2 lps remain on hook; cut color being used, leaving 4" end for weaving in later. With new color (leave 4" end) complete st (YO hook and pull though 2 loops on hook) = color changed.

THROW INSTRUCTIONS

With Color A, ch 194 loosely.

Row 1 (foundation row): Sc in 2nd ch from hook; *ch 3, skip 3 chs, sc in next ch; rep from * across, ch 1, turn.

Row 2 (pattern row): Sc in first sc; *ch 3, sc in next sc; rep from * across, ch 1, turn.

Rows 3 through 5: Rep Row 2, 3 times. At end of Row 5, change to Color B in last sc.

Repeat Row 2 in the following 12-row color sequence:

2 rows Color B

1 row Color A

1 row Color B

1 row Color A

2 rows Color B

5 rows Color A

Repeat the 12-row color sequence 7 times more. Finish off; weave in all ends securely.

LACY AND WARM

Finished Size: 36" x 54" (91.44 cm x 137.16 cm)

EASY

SHOPPING LIST

Yarn (Super Bulky) 6

[4 ounces, 64 yards (113 grams, 59 meters) per skein]

13 skeins

Crochet Hook

Size N (10 mm) crochet hook or size required for gauge

GAUGE INFORMATION

7 sc = 4" (10.16 cm)

THROW INSTRUCTIONS

Ch 77.

Row 1: Sc in 2nd ch from hook; *ch 5, skip next 2 chs, sc in each of next 2 chs; rep from * across to last 3 chs, skip next 2 chs, sc in last ch; ch 1, turn.

Row 2: *Work (4 sc, ch 5, 4 sc) in next ch-5 loop; rep from * across, ch 3, turn.

Repeat Row 2 until piece measures about 50" (127 cm); at end of last row, ch 1 instead of ch 3, turn.

Last Row: Sc in first sc; work 8 sc in each ch-5 loop across; sc in last sc. Finish off; weave in ends.

Turn work so right side is facing and foundation ch is at top. Join yarn in first st at right corner; work 6 sc in each ch-2 space across. Finish off; weave in ends.

PERFECT IN WHITE

Finished Size: 34" x 50" (86.36 cm x 127 cm)

EASY

SHOPPING LIST

Yarn (Super Bulky) 6

[3.5 ounces, 108 yards
(100 grams, 99 meters) per skein]
11 skeins Natural

Crochet Hook

Size N (10 mm) crochet hook or size required for gauge

GAUGE INFORMATION

6 sts = 2" (5.08 cm)

THROW INSTRUCTIONS

Ch 100 loosely.

Row 1 (right side): Sc in 2nd ch from hook and in each rem ch across: 99 sc, ch 3, turn.

Row 2: Skip first 2 sc, 2 sc in next sc; *ch 1, skip 2 sc, 2 sc in next sc; rep from * across, ch 3, turn.

Row 3: 2 hdc in each ch-1 space across, ending 2 hdc in space under turning ch, ch 3, turn.

Row 4: 2 sc in space between first two hdc groups, ch 1; *2 sc in space between next two hdc groups, ch 1; rep from * across, ending 2 sc in space under turning ch, ch 3, turn.

Rep Rows 3 and 4 until throw measures approx. 50" (127 cm) long, ending by working Row 4.

Last Row: Ch 1, turn; sc in each sc and in each ch-1 space across, ending sc in space under turning chain.

Finish off; weave in all ends.

GLORIOUS IN GREEN

Finished Size: 36" x 56" (91.44 cm x 127 cm)

EASY

SHOPPING LIST

Yarn (Bulky Weight) 5

[4 ounces, 124 yards (113 grams, 113 meters) per skein]
7 skeins

Crochet Hook

Size N (10 mm) crochet hook or size required for gauge

GAUGE INFORMATION

Shell = 1¼" (3.175 cm)

STITCH GUIDE

Shell: (dc, ch 1, dc) in st or sp indicated.

THROW INSTRUCTIONS

Ch 87 loosely.

Row 1: Sc in 2nd ch from hook and in each ch across: 86 sc; ch 3, turn.

Row 2: Skip 1 sc, Shell in next sc; *skip 2 sc, Shell in next sc, rep from * across to last 2 sts, skip 1 sc, dc in last sc; ch 1, turn.

Row 3: Sc in first st, work (sc, ch 1, sc) in each ch-1 sp across row to last st, sc in top of turning ch, ch 3, turn.

Row 4: Skip 1 sc, Shell in ch-1 sp; *skip 2 sc, Shell in next ch-1 sp, rep from * across to last 2 sc, skip 1 sc, dc in last sc; ch 1, turn.

Repeat Rows 3 and 4 for pattern until desired length, ending by working Row 4.

Last Row: Sc in each dc and ch-1 sp across. Finish off; weave in ends.

SOPHISTICATED CLOUDS

Finished Size: 34" x 46" (86.36 cm x 116.84 cm)

EASY

SHOPPING LIST

Yarn (Bulky Weight) 5

[6 ounces, 185 yards (170 grams, 169 meters) per skein]

5 skeins

Yarn (Medium Weight) 4

[3 ounces, 197 yards (85 grams, 180 meters) per skein]

2 skeins

Crochet Hook

Size K (6.5 mm) crochet hook or size required for gauge

GAUGE INFORMATION

10 sc = 4" (10.16 cm)

STITCH GUIDE

Reverse hdc: YO, insert hook into specified st to right, YO and pull up a loop, YO and draw through all 3 lps on hook: reverse hdc made.

THROW INSTRUCTIONS

With Bulky Weight yarn, ch 93 loosely.

Row 1: Sc in 2nd ch from hook and in each rem ch: 92 sc; ch 3 (counts as first dc of next row throughout), turn.

Row 2 (right side): Dc in next sc; *skip next sc, dc in next 3 sc, YO, insert hook in skipped sc and pull up a lp to height of a dc, (YO and draw through 2 lps) twice; rep from * across to last 2 sc, dc in last 2 sc; ch 1, turn.

Row 3: Sc in each st; ch 3, turn.

Rep Rows 2 and 3 alternately until piece measures about 44" (111.76 cm), ending by working a Row 3. At end of last row, ch 1 instead of ch 3, turn.

Border

Rnd 1: 3 sc in first sc for corner; sc across to last sc, 3 sc in last sc for 2nd corner; work even in sc around outer edges of throw, working 3 sc in each rem outer corner; join with a sl st to beg sc; finish off Bulky Weight yarn.

Rnd 2: Working now with two strands of Medium Weight yarn held tog, join yarn with sl st in center sc of any 3-sc corner group, ch 1, 3 sc in same st; work sc in each sc around, working 3 sc in center st of each 3-sc corner group; join in beg sc.

Rnd 3: Ch 1, sc in each sc around, working 3 sc in center st of each 3-sc corner group; join in beg sc.

Rnd 4: Ch 2; working now from left to right, skip next sc, ch 1; * reverse hdc in next sc to right, ch 1, skip next sc to right; rep from * around, join in first ch of beg ch-2. Finish off; weave in ends.

WARM AND WONDERFUL

Finished Size: 38" x 48" (96.52 cm x 121.92 cm)

EASY

SHOPPING LIST

Yarn (Bulky Weight)

[3.5 ounces, 129 yards (100 grams, 118 meters) per skein]

7 skeins

Crochet Hook

Size L (8 mm) crochet hook or size required for gauge

GAUGE INFORMATION

9 dc = 4" (10.16 cm)

THROW INSTRUCTIONS

Ch 83.

Row 1: Dc in 4th ch from hook (beg chs count as a dc) and in each rem ch: 81 dc, ch 4 (counts as a dc and ch-1 sp on following row), turn.

Row 2: *Dc in next dc, ch 1, sk next dc; rep from * across, ending dc in last dc, ch 4, turn.

Row 3: *Dc in next dc, ch 1, skip ch-1 sp; rep from * across, ending dc in last dc, ch 4, turn.

Row 4: Rep Row 3.

Row 5: *Dc in next dc, ch 1, skip ch-1 sp; rep from * across, ending dc in last dc, ch 3, turn.

Row 6: *Dc in next ch-1 sp, dc in next dc; rep from * across, ch 4, turn.

Rep Rows 2 through 6 until piece measures about 48" (121.92 cm), ending by working a Row 6. Finish off; weave in ends.

BRIGHT AND BEAUTIFUL

Finished Size: 30" x 48" (76.20 cm x 121.92 cm)

EASY

SHOPPING LIST

Yarn (Super Bulky) 6

[5 ounces, 87 yards (140 grams, 80 meters) per skein]

8 skeins

Crochet Hook

Size N (10 mm) crochet hook or size required for gauge

GAUGE INFORMATION

10 sc = 6" (15.24 cm)

THROW INSTRUCTIONS

Ch 61 loosely.

Row 1: Sc in 2nd ch from hook and in each rem ch: 60 sc, ch 1, turn.

Row 2: Sc in each sc, ch 1, turn.

Rows 3 through 5: Repeat Row 2.

Row 6: Sc in each sc, ch 3 (counts as first dc of next row throughout), turn.

Row 7: Dc in each sc, ch 1, turn.

Row 8: Sc in each dc, ch 3, turn.

Repeat Rows 7 and 8 until piece measures about 47" (119.28 cm) from beg ch, ending by working a Row 7. Work 6 rows in sc. Finish off; weave in all ends.

TRULY ELEGANT

Finished Size: 40" x 55" (101.60 cm x 139.7 cm)

EASY

SHOPPING LIST

Yarn (Bulky Weight) (5)

[3.5 ounces, 127 yards (100 grams, 116 meters) per skein]

Dark - 5 skeins
Medium - 4 skeins
Light - 4 skeins

Crochet Hook

Size L (8 mm) crochet hook or size required for gauge

GAUGE INFORMATION

12 dc = 5" (12.7 cm)

STITCH GUIDE

Shell: (2 dc, ch 2, 2 dc) in st or sp indicated.

Shell in Shell: Work shell in ch-2 sp of previous shell.

Long Double Crochet (long dc): Work dc in st or sp indicated 2 rows below, pulling up lp even with sts on hook: long dc made.

Long Double Crochet Cluster (long dc CL): Holding back last lp of each st, work 3 long dc in st or sp indicated 2 rows below, YO and draw through all 4 lps on hook: long dc CL made.

Decrease (dec): Holding back last lp of each st, work dc in each of next 2 sts indicated, YO and draw through all 3 lps on hook: dec made.

To change color: Work dc until 2 lps rem on hook, drop old color, pick up new color and draw through both lps on hook, cut dropped color.

THROW INSTRUCTIONS

With Dark, ch 91.

Row 1 (right side): Dc in 4th ch from hook and in next 3 chs; *shell in next ch, dc in next 5 chs, skip 2 chs, dc in next 5 chs; rep from * across to last 6 chs, shell in next ch, dc in last 5 chs; ch 3 (equals first dc of next row throughout), turn.

Row 2: Dec over next 2 dc, dc in 3 dc; *sk next dc, shell in shell, sk next dc, dc in 5 dc; skip 2 dc, dc in 5 dc; rep from * across, ending last rep with skip next dc, shell in shell, skip next dc, dc in 3 dc, dec over 2 dc, dc in 3rd ch of beg ch-3, changing to Medium in last st; ch 3 with new color, turn.

Instructions continued on page 24

Row 3: Dec over next 2 dc, dc in 2 dc; *long dc CL in skipped st 2 rows below, skip 2 dc, shell in shell; skip 2 dc, long dc CL in skipped st 2 rows below, dc in 4 dc, skip 2 dc, dc in 4 dc; rep from * across, ending last rep with long dc CL in skipped st 2 rows below, dc in 2 dc, dec over next 2 dc, dc in 3rd ch of turning ch; ch 3, turn.

Row 4: Rep Row 2, changing to Light in last st; ch 3, with new color, turn.

Row 5: Rep Row 3.

Continue to rep Rows 2 and 3, working two rows of each color, in sequence of Dark, Medium, and Light until piece measures about 55" (139.7 cm) long, ending by working a Row 2; at end of last row, ch 1, turn.

Edging

Rnd 1: 3 sc in first st, sc in 4 dc, skip next dc, 3 sc in ch-2 sp of shell, skip next dc, sc in 5 dc; *skip 2 dc, sc in 5 dc, skip next dc, 3 sc in ch-2 sp of shell, skip next dc, sc in 5 dc; rep from * across, ending last rep with sc in 4 sc, 3 sc for corner in last sc; working across long side edge, 2 sc in sides of rows, adjusting sts to keep work flat; at end of side, 3 sc in last st for corner; working in unused lps of beg ch, sc in each lp across, working 3 sc in peaks and 1 sc in valleys, 3 sc in last st for corner; work up long side as before, end with sl st in beg sc. Finish off; weave in all ends.

YARN INFORMATION

Throws in this book were made using a variety of yarns. Any brand of the specified weight of yarn may be used. It is best to refer to yardage/meters when determining how many balls to purchase.

For your convenience, listed below are the specific yarns used to create our photography models. Because yarn manufacturers make frequent changes in the their product lines, you may sometimes find it necessary to use a substitute yarn or to search for the discontinued product at alternate suppliers (locally or online).

SHINING SHELLS
Lion Brand® Lion's Pride® Woolspun®
#140 Violet

WONDERFUL WARMTH
Red Heart® Infinity®
#9351 Almond

SENSATIONAL STRIPES
Lion Brand® Wool-Ease® Chunky
Red - #189 Mulberry (A)
White - #099 Fisherman (B)

LACY AND WARM
Lion Brand® Hometown USA®
#222 Salem Creek

PERFECT IN WHITE
Bernat® Softee® Chunky™
28008 Natural

GLORIOUS IN GREEN
Lion Brand® Wool-Ease® Tonal
#171 Fern

SOPHISTICATED CLOUDS
Lion Brand® Homespun®
#600 Clouds
Lion Brand® Wool-Ease
#138 Cranberry

WARM AND WONDERFUL
Lion Brand® Wool-Ease® Thick & Quick®
#501 Sequoia

BRIGHT AND BEAUTIFUL
Lion Brand® Wool-Ease® Thick & Quick®
#507 Jungle

TRULY ELEGANT
Lion Brand® Lion's Pride® Woolspun®
Dark - #149 Charcoal
Medium - #147 Purple
Light - #150 Oxford Grey

GENERAL INFORMATION

ABBREVIATIONS

Crochet instructions are written with many abbreviations which helps keep printed instructions to a manageable length.
Here are the standard abbreviations used in these patterns:

Beg	beginning	Rem	remain (ing)
Ch (s)	chain (s)	Rep	repeat (ing)
Cl	cluster	Sc	single crochet
Dc	double crochet	Sk	skip
Dec	decrease	Sl st	slip stitch
Hdc	half double crochet	Sp (s)	space (s)
Hdc dec	half double crochet decrease	St (s)	stitch (es)
		YO	yarn over hook
Inc	Increase		
Lp (s)	loop (s)		

CROCHET TERMINOLOGY

The patterns in this book have been written using the crochet terminology used in the United States. Terms which may have different equivalents in other parts of the world are listed below.

United States	**International**
Gauge	tension
Skip	miss
Bind off	cast off
Slip Stitch	single crochet
Single Crochet	double crochet
Double crochet	Treble crochet

STITCHES

Slip Knot

Almost all crochet starts by first making a Slip Knot on the hook.

Step 1: Place yarn end on a flat surface, keeping a 6" end, and make a loop.

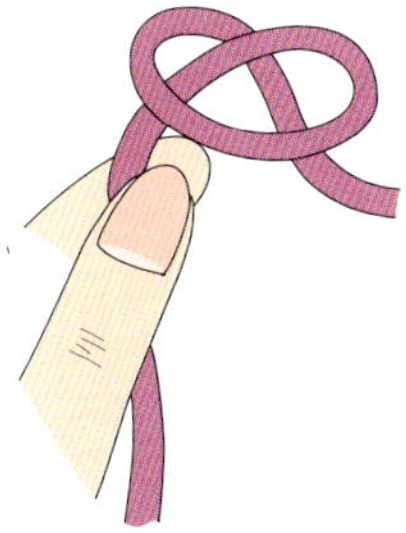

Step 2: Insert hook as shown and draw a lp up onto hook by pulling on end marked A. Slip Knot should slide easily on hook.

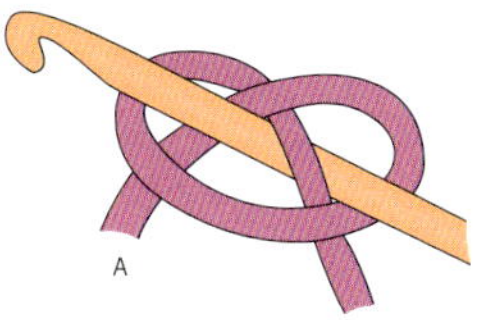

Make certain to leave loose yarn end 6" long for weaving in later.

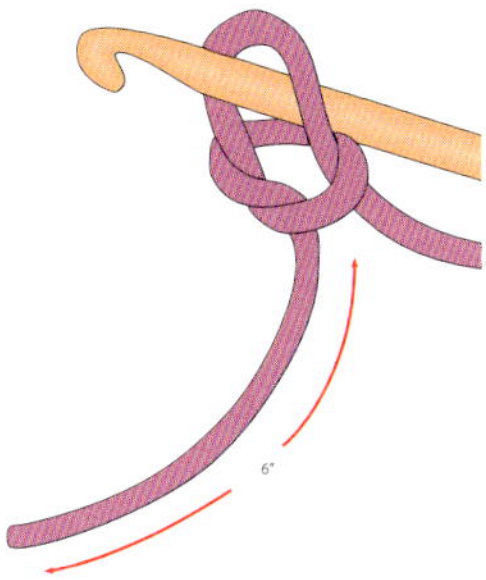

Foundation Chain

The starting point for all crochet worked in rows, the foundation chain should always be worked loosely. If you are a tight crocheter, use a hook one size larger than usual to make the chain.

Step 1: Make a Slip Knot on hook.

Step 2: Bring yarn from back to front over hook and draw it through lp on hook. You have now made one ch st.

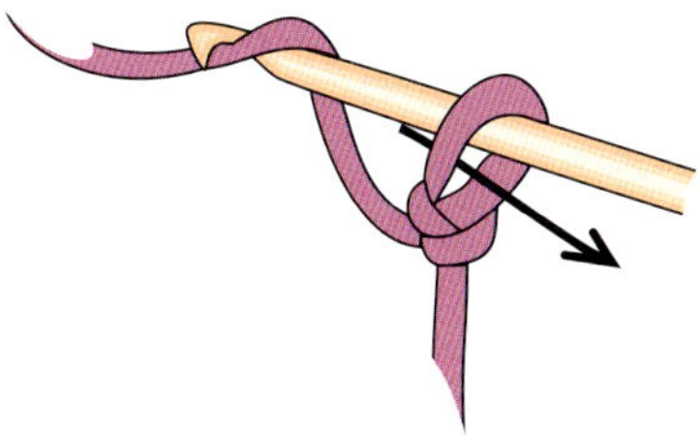

Step 3: Again bring yarn from back to front over hook and draw a through lp on hook. You have now made 2 ch sts.

Continue to rep step 3 until you have desired number of foundation chs.

Single Crochet

Single crochet is the shortest of the basic crochet stitches.

Step 1: Insert hook in specified ch or st and draw up a lp: 2 lps on hook.

Step 2: YO and draw hook through both lps on hook.

Single crochet (sc) completed.

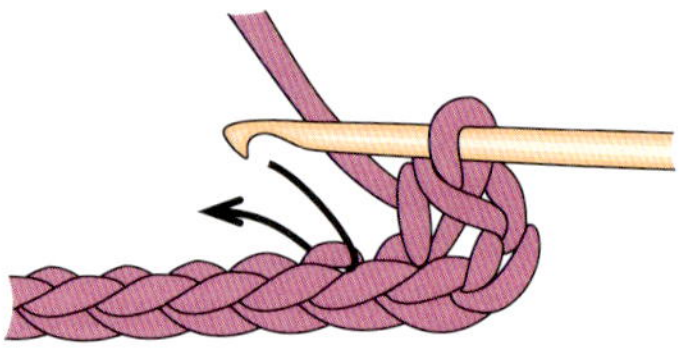

Double Crochet

Step 1: YO from back to front; skip first 3 chs from hook, and insert hook in back bump of 4th ch.

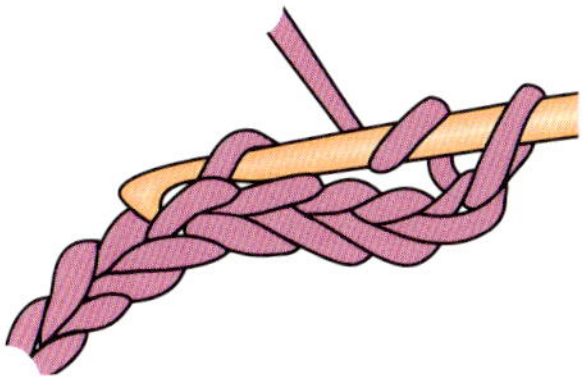

Step 2: YO and draw through ch st and up onto working area of hook: 3 lps rem on hook.

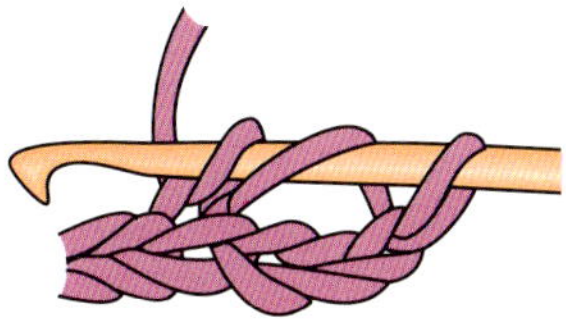

Step 3: YO and draw through first 2 lps on hook: 2 lps rem on hook.

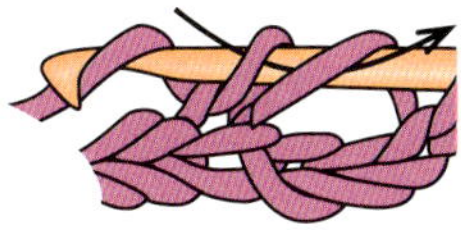

Step 4: YO again and draw through both lps on hook. You have now completed one double crochet (dc) st.

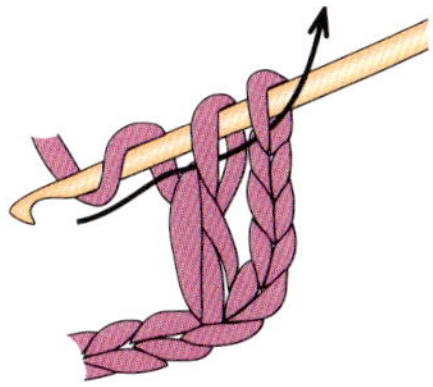

Half Double Crochet

A versatile crochet stitch that is slightly taller than single crochet and slightly shorter than double crochet. To work half double crochet, make the desired number of chains.

Step 1: YO; insert hook into 3rd ch from hook, YO and draw up lp: 3 lps now on hook.

Step 2: YO again and draw yarn through all 3 lps on hook at once; one half double crochet (hdc) is completed.

Rep steps 1 and 2 in each ch across row but in step 1, insert hook in next ch instead of 3rd ch from hook.

When turning hdc rows, 2 chs are usually used. They can be counted as first st of following row.

Slip Stitch

This stitch is used in four ways: to move yarn across an area without adding additional height, to join work at the end of a round of a piece worked in rounds instead of rows, to join new yarn, and to join seams.

Step 1: Insert hook in specified st, ch, or lp.

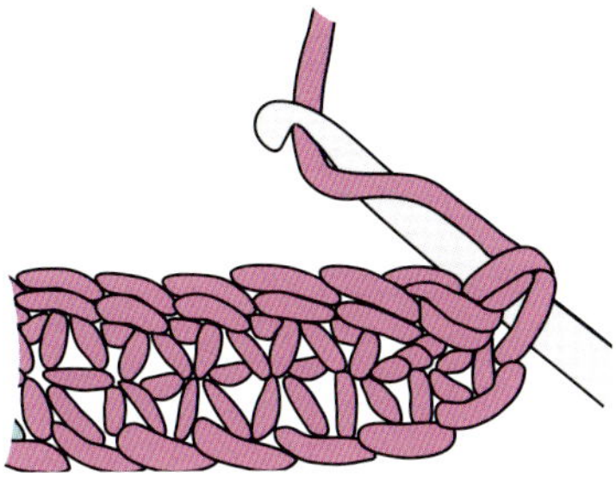

Step 2: YO and draw hook through both st, ch, or lp and lp on hook in one motion.

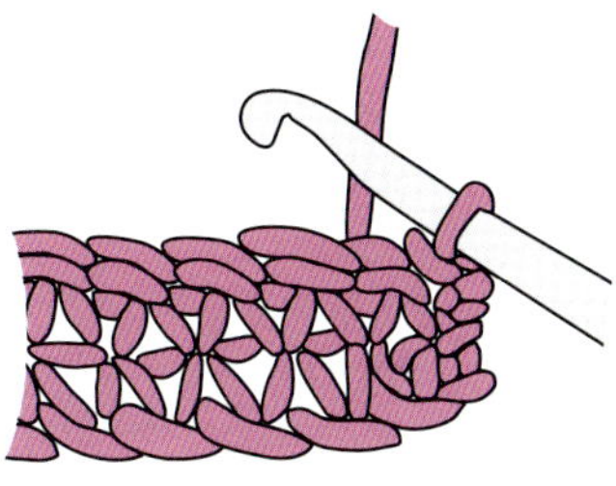

Finish Off

Term meaning to complete a piece by cutting the yarn, leaving a 6" end, and drawing the end through the last loop on the hook.

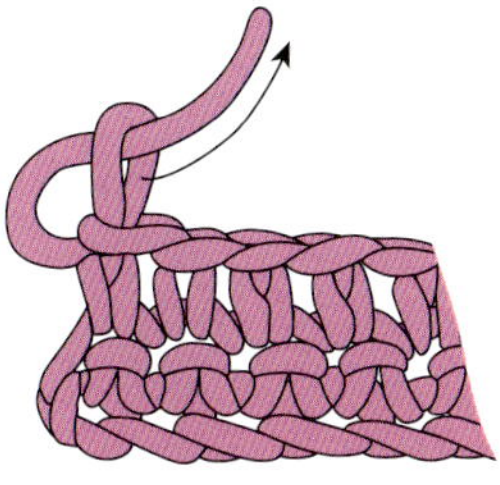

Skill Levels

Yarn manufacturers, publishers, needle and hook manufacturers have worked together to set up a series of guidelines and symbols to bring uniformity to patterns. Before beginning a project, check to see if your skill level is equal to the one listed for the project.

Beginner	Projects for first-time crocheters using basic stitches and minimal shaping.
Easy	Projects using yarn with basic stitches, repetitive stitch patterns, simple color changes, and simple shaping and finishing.
Intermediate	Projects using a variety of techniques, such as basic lace patterns or color patterns, mid-level shaping and finishing.
Experienced	Projects with intricate stitch patterns, techniques and dimension, such as non-repeating patterns, multi-color techniques, fine threads, small hooks, detailed shaping and refined finishing.

Yarn Weights

To make it easier for yarn manufacturers, publishers, and designers to prepare consumer-friendly products and for consumers to select the right materials for a project, the following standard yarn weight system has been adopted.

Standard Yarn Weight System

Categories of yarn, gauge, ranges, and recommended needle and hook sizes

Yarn Weight Symbol & Category	0 Lace	1 Super Fine	2 Fine	3 Light	4 Medium	5 Bulky	6 Super Bulky	7 Jumbo
Type of Yarns in Category	Fingering 10 count crochet thread	Sock Fingering, Baby	Sport, Baby	DK, Light, Worsted	Worsted, Afghan, Aran	Chunky, Craft, Rug	Super Bulky, Roving	Jumbo, Roving
Crochet Gauge* Ranges in Single Crochet to 4 inch	32-42 double crochets**	21-32 sts	16-20 sts	12-17 sts	11-14 sts	8-11 sts	6-9 sts	5 sts and fewer
Recommended Hook in Metric Size Range	Steel*** 1.6-1.4mm	2.25-3.5mm	3.5-4.5mm	4.5-5.5mm	5.5-6.5mm	6.5-9mm	9-16mm	16mm and larger
Recommended Hook US Size Range	Steel*** 6, 7, 8 Regular hook B-1	B-1 to E-4	E-4 to 7	7 to I-9	I-9 to K-10 1/2	K-10 1/2 to M-13	M-13 to Q	Q and larger

*GUIDELINES ONLY: The above reflect the most commonly used gauges and needle or hook sizes for specific yarn categories

**Lace weight yarns are usually crocheted on larger hooks to create lacy, openwork patterns. Accordingly, a gauge range is difficult to determine. Always follow the gauge stated in your pattern.

*** Steel crochet hooks are sized differently from regular hooks—the higher the number, the smaller the hook, which is the reverse of regular hook sizing.

Made in U.S.A.